DAYS LIKE LEAVES

Collected Poems by Andrew Buchanan

Arts Agency

Published in the United Kingdom
by The Arts Agency (2015)
ISBN 978-0-9564799-4-5

Andrew Buchanan has asserted his right under the Copyrights, Designs and Patents Act 1988 to be identified as the author of this work. Copyright ©Andrew Buchanan 2015.

All rights reserved. No part of this publication may be reproduced, stored in a retrieval system or transmitted in any for or by any means, electronic, mechanical, photocopying recording or otherwise, without the prior permission of the publisher. This book is sold subject to the conditions that is shall not, by way of trade or otherwise be lent, resold, hired out, or otherwise circulated without the publisher's prior consent in any form of binding or cover other than that in which it is published and without a similar condition including this condition, being imposed on the subsequent purchaser.

Other books published by The Arts Agency include:
'A Chain of Stars' by Sanae Morita. ISBN 978-0-9564799-0-7
Published and Designed by The Arts Agency
www.artsagency.co.uk

Dedicated to the Muses...

Contents

Even In Sleep	1
Listless and Anxious	2
Like An Apple from a Tree	3
Her Gaze	4
The First Time We Made Love	5
sunflowers and unicorns	6
I Think of You	7
Otherwise Engaged	8
Poem About a Painting	9
My Merchant Ships	10
The Last Romantic	11
Park Poem	11
Bird Life	12
Max Factor	13
Coming Home?	14
"The Barren Tender of a Poet's Debt"	16
Lovesick	17
The Belle of the Bank	18
African Nightfall	20
Winter Skies	21
On My island	22
And If This Heart	23
When into Strangers' Beds	24
A New Career In A New Town	26
Haiku	27

In times like these	28
A Contract of the Heart	29
In her Clandestine Fashion	30
And Just Because	32
The Measure of Her Heart	33
I caught a train	34
Poem Written While Drunk	36
Love is Blind	37
The Colours of Night	38
I Walked Past The Shop	39
No, but I used to…	40
My Days Crash Down	41
My Friend	42
This Young Girl	43
West of Eden	44
I See Her On The Train	46
These Arts of Indifference	47
This I Believe	48
Sunshine	50
This is My First Day Without You	51
Love and Loss	52
You Have My Heart	54
Bamboo	56
He's Holding Out For Heaven	58
Concupiscence	60

Even in Sleep

And you my love
sleeping beside me
soft shoulders
above white sheets
tousled blond curls
on the curve of your cheek
seem utterly removed
vulnerable yet complete
yet you curl around me
even in sleep

Listless and Anxious

Listless and anxious
We remonstrate with the past
invest in longing
and court time

Like An Apple From a Tree

Like an apple from a tree
her love hung there
just for me

And like a boy
I carelessly stole it
thinking it a thing
of so little consequence
that a love so sweetly given
would always be there
for the taking

But like an apple from a tree
her love now hangs
just out of reach

Her Gaze

My temples thud
my pulse it races
that a stranger's glance
can make me feel this way

but something deep
transforms her gaze
in one so young
an air so grave

The First Time We Made Love

The first time we made love
You came to me
cool, sleek, and wild

moving to me
under the covers
shivering slightly
though whether through
the cold or the moment
I could not tell

And while taking
intimate liberties
in our secret darkness
I was taken aback
by your passion,
how you cried when you came
and then held me ferociously close
as if having made me your own
you would not let me go

sunflowers and unicorns

your hands caress
cooing white doves
you wade
thigh deep in furs
straddle light
nectar of peaches
my bones shall
be your flutes

I Think of You

I think of you
most days

of the things
you would say
of the things
we would do

how your body would turn
this way and that
to give and take
our mutual pleasure
Though others have
loved me more
I have wanted them less

My wildest child
your passion
from abandoned
to abandonment

still sears me
even across
all these years

Otherwise Engaged

Your phone call
across all these years
took me by surprise
You called to tell me
you were getting married
When I was with you
I didn't want to marry
But now

I do ?

Poem about a Painting

In her marble chamber
she sits against a pillar
one shoulder bared above
her silk chemise
betrays her deep indifference

her tamed wildbirds
her fountains
are lost upon her now
our lady is disconsolate
her servant slips away

her mood is as inconsolable
as the damson that she wears
she is resigned to her surroundings
but her sadness still remains

My Merchant Ships

My merchant ships
Tug at the harbour
Bales of silk
Arabian amber

A porcelain mask
My epitaph.

The Last Romantic

the last romantic
dreams in libraries
cascading curls
victorian lace
bright wide eyes
gentle face

Park Poem

Couple on bench
nestled laughing
sharing warm secrets

fallen leaves
between blades
forever

Bird Life

My falcon flies
high in the skies
then swoops,
and claws and kills

My humming birds
around these flowers
float faster than these bees

My night owls
above the crowds
sagaciously serene

Max Factor

Eyes as wide
as blue lagoons
lashes soft as
pillow feathers

she arches her brow
like a dove's wing
in flight
levels her gaze
to an indolent pout

lifts frosted fingernail
to high gloss lip
kisses her cigarette
 - my heart just went flip

Coming Home?

My favourite city
is the city of
The Bell, The Book,
The Fish and The Star

At night my city is
strung with lights
hung with stars

A fresh rain falling
guzzled by car fumes
christens my city anew

And perusing
faded phone numbers
and anonymous addresses
leafing through lives
neglected or forgotten
though the years lie between us
like rows of unread diaries
I will come to call
as awkward and eager as ever

And passing through your cities
as I seem to pass through my life
perhaps someday
I'll find somewhere and stay

So that I who have
visited your lives
can let you visit mine

**"The Barren Tender of
a Poet's Debt" (Shakespeare)**

All my hopes
caught in her glance
sleepless longing
my recompense

Her beauty hurts
glows in ashes
eclipses my days
with a hopeless passion

I'd die of love
but contented be
if her sweet face
were turned to me

Lovesick

Like the
sweetest fever
I cannot kick
this dream
of you

that suffuses
my life
with longing
but will not
leave me

as you
have done

The Belle of the Bank

Miss Amanda Beach
Miss Amanda Beach
She's the belle of the bank
with an ass like a peach

She's always smiling
whomsoever she greets
She's groomed and she's sweet
And her handwriting's neat

Miss Amanda Beach
Please don't tell me I'm spurned
is it too much to hope
to have my interest returned?

I pop in to the branch
with some lighthearted quip
about investment broking
in the post-keynsian dip

But the way that you look
makes me feel so perplexed
I've started dreaming at night
about the Dowe Jones Index

I want a current account
not her final demand
But I cherish each chit
that is writ by her hand

African Nightfall

a black face in a blue turban
bougainvillea and jacaranda

she's as
bright as a wave

she's got
leo's favours

Winter Skies

Grey winter clouds
flatten the sky
taking even the
last cold sunlight

Black storm clouds
scudding across the sky
rumbling about like vast armadas
threatening war in heaven

On My Island

I tell myself it's not her
It's just a need we all have
that any form or face might do
and not just hers

But I who thought myself
immured against the tides of the heart
and their constant turnings
between love and its sense of loss
Now find myself
caught in deeper currents
tugged at the heart
as if having admitted to love
I now become vulnerable to its loss

So that I who thought
that I could give love
without asking for any in return
now find myself
seeking her grace and favour
like a puppet on love's strings

And If This Heart

And if this heart
is an island

she climbed ashore
unnoticed

breached my
battered seas walls
charmed their
bricks and mortar

and appeared on
the other side

as if to say
how easy it could be
to reach me

and how
nice it is
to be reached

When into Strangers' Beds

When into
strangers' beds she falls
seeking only
that comfort which
catch as she can
may not diminish
against the
coming of the night

Yet it's not
love's assassins
stalking the dark corners
of her heart
for her love
needs no reasons
or no alibis

and in the
gentle darkness
under the blankets
it seems possible
to believe in anything
even in him

but something
buried deep inside her
whispers
for love you gave
yourself away
a price she knows
he will not pay

A New Career in a New Town

I want to stay up late
in a brand new town
feel the rain beating
against my windowpane
urgent, like my heart

Haiku

Warm and snug
Curled in his winter shell
- a sleeping slug

Her summer dress
blue flowers on white snow
stops just above
the back of her knee

I hurried home
in case you'd called
but on my ansaphone
no messages I want to hear

In times like these

In times like these
when nowhere is better
than anywhere
and all roads
lead to here

And time is a memory
our yesterdays
a sweet blur
that own us
through and through
try as we may

Or time is a dream
our scattered vanities
on which we paint tomorrow
emblematic tatters
to keep out the cold

sad creatures
we fall back
into ourselves
fall like rain

A Contract of the Heart

You come to me
vulnerable and open
like a sister or a lover
I have been waiting
to meet for years

You have travelled so far
and come to me so quickly
so little known
and yet so close

Then you tell me
you have to go back
home on tomorrow's flight

Stunned by love
then suddenly
I'm stunned again by its loss

But perhaps there is a greater distance
between two people
And although we may be
continents apart
we've made a contract of the heart

In her Clandestine Fashion

From her nose stud
to her anklet
from her designer dress
to her donkey boots

Her hennaed hair
swept to one side
across her eyelashes
styled in seventies chic
piled high on top
but shaved at one side
her plaits
straggling artfully
down the sides and
nape of her neck

She carries
wrapped around her
her own mystery

But in her eyes
she holds
evidence of reasons,
promises and secrets

Because I want her only
but she isn't mine
we meet in a clandestine fashion
steal time and kisses
in unequal measure
against the encroaching hours

She's the sweetest thing I've seen
I want no-one as much as her
My secret lover
we touch and don't tell
- that's her clandestine fashion

And Just Because

And just because
she calls me
I can think of
no better reason
than to stay

And just because
She holds me
I can ask no more of her
than that she stays

And just because
she kisses me
her lips seeking mine
against all the odds

That my world and all its
myriad small confusions
can be turned to something
as simple and sweet as this

The Measure of Her Heart

The measure of her heart
is not so great that she would
lose her composure
and come running to me only

Yet the measure of her heart
is not so small
that she would
willingly lose me
to return to her own

Perhaps the measure of her heart
is that she has lost a little of it
to both of us
but in her turnings
between duty and desire
has not lost her head.

**I caught a train that passed through
the town where you lived**

Our romance began on a platform
A goodbye kiss that went on
rather longer than expected
filled with an urgency occasioned by
our otherwise restrained politenesses
and the imminent departure
of my train

The next time
you met me on the train
"I've got away" you confided,
"and watched The Chart Show"

as we set off on
our Saturday expedition
like the perfect Network Southeast
advertisement for the
romance of the railways

And now
when I pass through your city
half hoping for a glimpse of you
out of the window

I marvel how one can lose something
one has never really owned
and still miss it so

Poem Written While Drunk

I got drunk tonight
and thought of you

thought of
seeing you again
this weekend

And though I was alone
my friends too far,
too broke, or too pregnant

when I thought of you
life's sweet expectancy
reclaimed my drunken heart

Love is Blind

These flowers are not
for her eyes
their true colours are
unknown to us
strange ultraviolet flags
for eyes other than ours

And as the bee
is also duped by the flower
to carry pollen
still we try
confused by love
and try again
to sense what's real

sweet victims of biology
which makes
blind fools
of us all

The Colours of Night

Walking home
late one night
the trees are
arced in orange
street light

the colours of night are
iridescent amber and
translucent inky black blue

I Walked Past The Shop

I walked past the shop
where I'd bought the flowers
for your Birthday

What message do you want
on the card?
she'd said

What could I say?

After five years
two of them apart
and now no more

Send them with my love
seems too little and
yet so much to say

No, but I used to ...

Chromatic rainbows
in faded grey

Elegant phrases
forgotten care

Black marks on white paper
call up the colours of the heart

Lullabye oblivion
my forgotten arts

My Days Crash Down

My days
crash down
around me
silent waves
in unperpetual motion

My time
slips past
unnoticed
like water flowing
under a frozen river

I trace the
arc of the wind
in the gull's flight
and wonder

How strange to forget
when it
burns like a fuse
inside us all

My Friend

My friend
she's shy and sweet

But when she's happy
she dances in the street

And each time she smiles
all the joy spills out in the world

And each time she laughs
it's like a shadow is lifted
from my heart

This Young Girl

This young girl
with unspoilt eyes

who laughes your life
awake from sleep

will not wait
nor want for long

her youthfulness
is your remorse

West of Eden

She gave me
three red apples
and smiled at me

She'd held up the entire queue
and when the apples arrived
and weren't good enough for her
she sent them back to be changed
like an imperious Persian Princess

She had remembered
I had left behind an apple
in the store a year ago,
and had even remembered
it was a red apple

This girl from Iran
to Asda checkout
whose name means Morning Light
whom I do not know,
but would like to

One for you
One for me
One for something
that's not to be

So near,
so far
Sahar

I See Her On The Train

I see her on the train
I do not know her name
We talk but not for long
she chats and then is gone

Dark eyed and clever
intelligent and neat
Dark haired and lovely
she's all I want to meet

What is it that I feel
that makes my life unreal?
Except when seeing her
my days are just a blur

Just how can it be
that she means so much to me?
That this girl I do not know
has captured me so

I saw her on the train
I did not know her name
And now she is not there
My life has lost all care.

These Arts of Indifference

These arts of indifference
so carefully cultivated
to hide one's care

It's as if affection
or interest, or curiosity,
are a sign of weakness
a hint of intimacy
might scare her away

Yet with her
I'm pleased to be silent
having nothing to say
I am happy to share it

Yet now apart
the days seem still and empty
one's familiar surroundings
suddenly chill

This I Believe

I have no faith
in superstitious rites
nor will I bow or bend
or kneel in prayer

no sacred books
no holy place
no sutras, psalms
no saving grace

no special God
looking out for me
while million die
of poverty

no popes or priests
no vicars for me
instead I'll invite
Richard Dawkins for tea

no crystals, angels,
dreams or destinies
no panpipes, readings
or 'spirituality'

I'll work and try
to find my place
just you and me
the human race

Sunshine

As the shining sun
sinks beneath the rooftops,
leaving my garden
bereft of basking in its
soft warm light

I turn indoors,
a little sad, but still grateful,
for another day of my life
sitting in my little corner of the earth,
under the golden light of heaven

This is My First Day Without You

This is my first day without you

No more tiptoeing through the house
No more strange food left out for me
when I come home late

No more musically lilting language
or subtitled tv
No more excitable chatter
and girlish laughter

No more wet haired slim brown body
back from the shower

I come home to a dark house,
and a room, suddenly empty,
like my heart.

Love and Loss

Reading all your old emails to me again
In the early hours of the morning
I realise I never
wrote a poem about you
Never wrote how you made me feel

But perhaps sometimes
Love is so complicated
Life is so complicated
Loss is so complicated
That it cannot easily be reduced
into simple stanzas

Still, now we are five years apart
Perhaps it is now almost
manageable in words
at least the outward form
if not the inner ache

And so, whenever I have lost my way
Or love has become a stranger to me
I stay up late and
I reread your cards and emails to me
Look at your photos

Remember what we were to each other
and what we weren't

And my heart remembers
Love will survive time
will survive loss,
and the cares of the ordinary world

You Have My Heart

Though you have
another husband
and a new baby
You have my heart

Though you now live
on the other side of the world
continents apart
You have my heart

Though we only have
furtive phonecalls
and urgent emails
You have my hears

Though I barely knew you
Time has closed this gap
You have left with all my longing
You have my heart

Though I did not realise it
Right from the start
I cannot love another
You have my heart

Though we had to little time
And now we are apart
You are closer to me than anyone
You have my heart

For love crosses all borders
Shakes everything apart
And like a thief in the night
You have my heart

Bamboo

My bamboo plant
a present from you
is yellowing and dying

I've kept it for a long time
after you've gone
in memory of you
An innocent abroad,
before you ran back home
away from a loveless marriage
made to appease your family,
a husband who stole your money,
and a stateless child you loved.

I think I didn't water it often enough
And, when I did, I watered it
too much.

I think I must have neglected you too
while you waited in this country,
not wanting to go back home,
not wanting to stay here,
waiting for me to help you

Ah, now you have disappeared
back into a country full
of nearly one and a half billion people.

I'm so sad I didn't do more,
and I hope your new life
is better than here.

He's Holding Out For Heaven

Well, he's holding out for heaven
just a little bit would do
Where the summer rains are sweeter
and the skies are bluest blue

Where the world turns in real time
and for all tomorrow's parties
For truth and beauty and love
for people kinder and smarter

For the girl who understands
who makes his heart beat faster
For now and ever after
for the sound of children's laughter

Although he's had his share of chances
of lovers left to languish
Something deep inside has always said
this is not where your heart lies

But as tomorrow becomes yesterday
and the sand in the glass runs faster
He knows he should
take hold of his life
As the days blow by like
leaves in the storm

Well, he's holding out for heaven
just a little bit would do……

Concupiscence

I thought my heart a broken toy
discarded, flawed and incomplete
So now I roam from life to life
in search of something sweeter

So if you see me looking
at you don't worry
I'm just trying to capture your beauty
curious at how precious and rare it is
like (fragments of) summer stars

www.ingramcontent.com/pod-product-compliance
Lightning Source LLC
Chambersburg PA
CBHW020021050426
42450CB00005B/584